ODD MAN OUT

Poems about School Life –
and Life after School

Frank Rose

First published in Great Britain by Pen Press an
Imprint of Indepenpress Publishing Ltd
25 Eastern Place
Brighton
BN2 1GJ

ISBN 978-1-907172-49-6

Printed and bound in the UK

A catalogue record of this book is available from
the British Library

Cover design Jacqueline Abromeit

Dedications

For David, Shirley, and Yvonne.

About the Author

Frank Rose was for many years the
headmaster of a London junior school.

Contents

PART ONE

LIFE AFTER SCHOOL

BIRTHDAY PARTY

The passing thought was worth, I thought,
        a passing thought.

Ducks started it, mating on the morning Lee.
She, poor drab thing, subjected to some indignity,
        All but submerged,
Emerged shaking; surged ahead making, finally free,
A fine cascade… a shade too unconcerned for me.
        Strangely, I pitied.
Warmed by an unexpected glow of expansive piety,
I pitied brute minds that make gross for most
        What matters most
More than cute mindless brutes who blindly mate.

Later at the birthday party, a toast: To Host! –
        Health! – Life itself! And
A choice of choice roast bird; a chance to flatter
Those who matter. (All matter? No matter.
        Who matter most.)

So, step by step, lights to Light, gold to Gold,
Arm in arm, to where gold-downed day-old ducklings
        – So sweet! –
Startled by strange feet, cut off from their gold
Dawn-lit water retreat, filled us with chuckling delight
        And a smug warm afterglow –
For after all, we too must be really rather sweet,
        And rather deep;
And, yes, spiritual, to sense in things so small
The magical – the mystical – the greater Whole! –

3

Each linked to each;
We too linked to each, we part of the Whole...
Which is why we can pity. Ducks started it all.

That passing thought? Worth, I thought,
            a passing thought.

OCTOBER GIRL –
reading Eliot outside Hampstead tube station

October girl leans beside
Shadows of October days;
Glances up, wide-April-eyed,
To meet my shy October gaze
Where the sad leaves yellow glide
Into web-drawn amber rays.

October girl looks up and sees –
Sees and understands –
Balding by the balding trees
Wistfulness that stands,
Trousers rolled up to his knees,
Coffee spoon in hands.

Autumn girl with autumn hair
Where the tired leaves dance,
What poems have spoken where
Eyes met eyes by chance!
Epics in a single stare,
Lyrics in a glance.

Eyes that linger soon resign
To go their separate ways:
October girl to hers, not mine,
April in her gaze;
Prufrock's to the Northern Line
Where a sea-girl strays.

THE PLEASURE OF YOUR COMPANY

A last glance in the mirror, a final finger
On the zip… and too late to bunk off now.
Time to pass among the Guests, star-scattered
On the grass – a swami here, a rabbi there –
Bathed in sweat and oozing fraternity.

Sherry and salted peanuts only. Speeches
To follow. Drift dry-mouthed; face, aching
From smiling, colliding with faces smiling.
Admire a tree. Examine a rose. Other faces
Glow with grace and evening sunlight.

Our concern is Peace, Love, a second sherry,
And the plight of a world that weeps.
A Conference planned: 300 delegates (applause)
From 39 countries: Muslims, Buddhists, Jains, Jews…
Don't clap, you fool, clasping sherry.

Our concern is Human Rights! – *don't clap!* –
Education! Survival! (Above all, survival.)
And they are good people, all. The Right Rev.
Is such a good man. The girl in open sandals
Is so pretty. Why am I not a good man?

Later at the lakeside café a different peace:
A curtain of willows by lapping water.
To open the cream peel back the lid. Squeeze.

Trousers ruined… the coffee remains black.
Think of things spiritual. Shantih.
                              Shalom.
                                   Tamám.

COME INTO THE GARDEN, ALL

The gardeners, at last they've gone;
    No more hoes, ho ho! s, or hoses.
I am alone with Maud and Tennyson –
    Alone in my Eden with roses.

A woman's cry! – not from Maud's lips.
    A weary refrain of despair:
'Eat up your chips!… Eat up your chips!'
    Intrudes like a rhythmic prayer.

Small sticky fingers probe, explore;
    Faces peer with running noses.
But I came to hide, to dream, to adore –
    Lost in a garden with roses.

Where better to dream? Rivulets fall,
    Traffic is muted, lilies unfold.
The larkspur listens… Again the call! –
    'Your chips are getting cold!'

'Eat, little angels,' the roses all sigh:
    Angels with della Robbia faces.
'Eat up, you buggers!' – Mother's cry –
    'Not that man's shoelaces.'

Alone once more, I am here at the gate
    With passion flowers and roses.
A rustle. Footsteps. 'Sorry, mate,
    Time!' The garden closes.

BY TREES BEREAVED

'These bloody leaves get on your bloody nerves,'
    the sweeper said.
'This is only the beginning,' I said to comfort him.

Leaves and your laughter define the moment... leaves
    like snow drifting into the corners of morning.

'Look,' I said, 'this leaf the shape of your heart.
    See, I hold your heart in my hands.'

'Each leaf,' you said, 'once spring, soon dust...
    And my heart, a leaf in your hands...'

'This is only the beginning,' I said to comfort you.

FLESH AND 6 PIGMENTS

I was not looking at the girl in the painting
But at the girl looking at her – and thinking,
In ten years from now only one will be as fresh,
As limpidly lovely, as now – but no more;
Only as demure, as doe-eyed, as quiescent,
As frozen, as barren, as now.

NEVER-NEVER LAND

In Hyde Park today
a hare sidled up towards us,
cat-black, November-slim,
watching us, not in wonder,
as we watched him,
but in his leporine way
pleased, I think, to see us.
– A black hobnobbing hare
taking in its languid stride
the South Kensington air?

Of course I soon understood
what had happened. Beside
the Serpentine, out of sight,
the Frampton statue stood:
rabbits, fairies, Timeless Boy
stuck there day and night
in all weathers. What if,
after posing 90 years,
one rabbit, bored stiff,
whispered into fairy ears?

Common sense? Cold logic?
Call it what you will. But –
try telling it to children!
They, being small,
still believed in Magic…
and Magic was to stare
at a mild-mannered, tame -
wild, real-life hare,

11

close-up – or at all –
lunching by the Albert Hall.

LILAC TIME

Better our paths had never crossed –
I who cannot hurt a fly, you embossed
On pale lilac posing no threat easily defined
    – Just there. And the impending cost
Of your visit? I am by nature more inclined
To prefer the company of my own kind
When it comes to sharing bedrooms.

In the next room my son sleeps.
He is young; too young to know he keeps
My rules about the sanctity of life: grand
Pious stuff. Whatever crawls or creeps
He carries to safety. He wouldn't understand
Why somewhere between Spain and Swaziland
My encyclopedia has spotless pages.

What is there to expiate? – to justify?
I kill… and sleep; or I spare… and lie
Awake, afraid to dream. You who loom
So large on pastel, I who cannot hurt a fly,
Share too little so too much: this lilac room
And life – at both ends of a kitchen broom.
Why didn't you stay in the cellar?

A PROMISE KEPT

The seagull adjusted
his spectacles, and gazing
coldly at me said he trusted
I did not mind his raising
a matter which had caused
him and his flock much distress.
Pointedly he paused.
Patiently I waited unable to guess
what was coming. As I knew,
he went on, some of his kind
wintered in town, flew
from coasts hoping to find
in human habitat the wherewithal
to keep body and soul together.
'Bird and man! – aren't we all
flesh and blood and feather?'

Soul? I mused. Has man a soul?
Wisely I uttered no word,
uncertain of the protocol
when lectured by a bird.

Now he felt compelled to protest,
speak out! – his voice shrill.
'Man feathers his own nest;
birds must keep a stiff upper bill
exposed to human greed –
but this!' - he waved a claw –
'this notice, *Please Do Not Feed
The Gulls*, sticks in the craw.

Speciesism!' Did I not see?
(I looked the word up later on
but thought it prudent to agree.)
Glasses off, his eyes shone
like yellow beads in snow,
unblinking in sustained attack:
'Gulls greedy! Pot-bellied crow
calling the kestrel black!
Ha! *"Dinner, dear, tonight?*
Halibut steak or lemon sole?
Flying so whets the appetite."
Do not feed the gulls! – oh droll!
Take breakfast!' (I had of course
but he was in no mood for puns.)
'Prerogative of cat, dog, horse;
man's pets: the favoured ones.
Our breakfast if it ever comes –
a gull should have the luck –
consists of leftovers, crumbs,
from banquets for the duck.'

A broody silence, broken by cries
from colleagues above.
   Could he tell
by my reluctance to meet his eyes
that I had breakfasted rather well? –
Pure juice (no coffee), muesli,
eggs, pancakes, waffles, glacé plums,
a pastry or two, Earl Grey tea
(no sugar)… and he on crumbs!
   Sensing my unease,
the seagull softened. His task –
to pass on the impassioned pleas
of peckish peers – completed, he'd ask

15

now only that I convey his profound
volucrine message to humankind.
I asked if verse would do. He frowned.
Simple rhyme he did not mind,
but, '...kindly avoid obscurity lest
one opens up a can of worms.'
I promised I would do my best.
We parted on good terms.

A FAMILY CRISIS

All right, not a crisis, but what do you do?
A bird built her nest on the ledge of the loo.
Fuss? Joy? Excitement? I tried to curb it
When David said, 'Poor thing, we mustn't disturb it.
We'll walk on tiptoe and speak in a hush,
Not open the window or work the flush –
Well there's hers next door, why can't we share?
She uses our lawnmower. It's only fair.'

Shirley, who's practical, only partly agreed:
'Yes, but what's greater, the bird's or our need?
If it's weeks before the fledglings take flight
Then it could be awkward, especially at night.'
   Yvonne, nearly 6, said, 'Let's bring it inside
To be safe and warm, with the door open wide.'
Lavatories, she thought, were lonely places.
'It would be lovely to see baby bird faces.'

The matter was solved, in fact, by the bird.
She wasn't offended. I doubt if she heard.
But she flew off this morning and hasn't returned,
For her own convenience – and all concerned.

RUSTY

Parents unknown.
Streetwise from the start. Take
His lead from the hook in the hall
And you'd count yourself lucky
Not to be simultaneously washed,
Knocked down, trampled on. Manners?
Yawned like a crocodile, scratched
Like a prospector nosing out gold,
Snapped at bluebottles: always missed.
A life without refinement.

Chased all cats –
Provided they scooted first, like
Birds or squirrels. A cavalry charge!
Then back, eyes shining like lamps.
But if a cat coldly stood its ground
The brakes would go on fast.
A triumphant return all the same.
It's no use wagging your tail, I'd say.
What are you so pleased about?
Like talking to the wall.

One wild day
When he was nearly 13 and nearly
Respectable, he let himself out and
Never returned. The man on the phone
Said the man in the car couldn't
Put the brakes on fast enough.
    I walk with him still, talk to him,
Explain things. I'm never alone.

18

The birds and cats just ignore him.
His lead still hangs in the hall.

AS I SAID TO THE LORD MAYOR OF FOWEY...

Name dropping is hard.
Try saying Kierkegaard –
(Wrong!) Or Antiochus Epiphanes.
Epi/phanes? Epiphah/nes? –
Stiffer knees? Bananas?
You feel such an ignoramus
Partying with the rich and famous,
Who make the glossy magazines,
When they're busy praising Keynes
And you think... No one explains.
It's all those ay's and ee's.
Caius, if you please, is keys.
Yeats is Yates
But Keats isn't Kate's.
No, name dropping's no fun.
Calling Donne Don isn't done,
Cowper wasn't Cow but Coo,
Roosevelt preferred Roe to Roo,
Wodehouse? – not Wode but Wood,
St John is Sinjin. Sinjin's Wood?
You can't win, it's no good.

The one I feel most sorry for
(Apart from Sory Kierkegaard)
Is that poor Mrs Goethe.
I mean, it must hurt her,
The names they call her boy –
As I said to the Lord Mayor of Fowey.

MOMENTS OF EQUALITY

Face to face with white tiles,
The professor of philosophy smiles
At me. Sudden buddies, we chat
About the weather, this and that;
No Wittgenstein, no Schopenhauer:
The Language Game of status, power,
Goes with gold braid, cap and gown.
Try playing it with trousers down!

I learnt this in the Arabian Sea
When a half-bald head fortuitously
Bobbing beside mine engaged my head
In pithy pleasantries instead
Of the usual ritualised pap. 'Sir'
Sounded wrong. Situations confer
Rank. Bare bodies confronting seas
Acknowledge other authorities.

BETRAYAL

You never fail to be surprised,
as the false gods topple one by one about you,
that what seems or claims to be is not What Is.
You never fail to be hurt that What Is is not
what they promised would be.

Those early giants in whose shadows
they trained you to walk, those later deities
you taught yourself to worship, who were they
really? Their light ever shining in your eyes,
blinded, you could not see.

Who, if it comes to that (and often
it comes to that), is the uniquely favoured
ubiquitous figure, untoppled, always forgiven,
who stares back with steadfast eyes? – he and
you, partners in conspiracy.

MOUSEHOLE

Walking downhill from the Wild Bird Sanctuary
To the small stone harbour where free birds fly
Over gold sands, and golden-skinned children play
By a sea that is not this calm cobalt every day,
I see painted just beneath the LADIES sign
The appendage LIFE MEANS NOTHING. A wry line
Playfully positioned? A genuine cry of despair?
Either way, you don't expect to find it there.
She – if a she – might have picked, after all,
The Lifeboat Station or the Sanctuary wall.

*In December 1981 the Penlee Lifeboat was lost with all
hands while engaged in a rescue mission in atrocious
weather conditions. All 8 members of crew lived at
Mousehole.*

SPRINGFIELD PARK –
London E5

As far as youth and old age go,
The great dividing line is snow.
I'm getting on now (over 30)
And still don't find snow dangerous, dirty.
Fall flakes! – my daughter on my lap;
Bridge the generation gap.

*

We stood before this Hackney hill unscarred
By ice: sledge and laughter got the edge on snow.
Arm in arm, those bleak black poplars barred
Our wild forced entry into Walthamstow.

*

Yellow crocus, white grass,
Step aside and let me pass.
I have some business at the zoo
With animals to interview;
Morning's frosted filigree,
Sunlit, cuts no ice with me.
Unhand me, will you, Yellowhead.
Pick on someone else instead.

*

Then suddenly… this tree
Lording it over daffodils;

Stealing, so it seemed to me,
The high notes of morning's song.
It was too cold to stay for long.

*

In the springtime of the year
The cherry tree shampoos her hair
And no one thinks it rude to stare.
But after that who comes to see,
For 12 months more, the cherry tree?

*

I sang May's tune
Before I knew the words:
Blown blossom strewn
Over dead baby birds.

*

At first nobody noticed the spawn,
But later the ditch was filled with shoals
Of squirming tadpoles. Their spring-dawn
Battle raged till early summer: tadpoles
Versus
Nets, jars, plastic bags, barking dogs.
Nature, not Man, said: Let there be frogs.

*

Summer. Attention settles
On butterflies, not nettles –
Briefly. A 2-fold sting:

Unfolded leaf, folded wing.

*

These flowers, you say, should never die.
But why? To flower is to begin to die –
Each perfect bloom, and you and I…
The evergreen is ever dead: never seen,
        never said…

*

How can beauty be truth,
Truth beauty? Keats is beauty caught;
Kant, truth sought. Beauty pleases, truth teases.
Beauty flirts – kisses – delights.
Thought hurts – misses – excites.
Birds may be true **and** beautiful. Wasps aren't.
Words may make beauty of truth or lies:
Keats can. Kant can't.

*

'Sorry, little fellow,
No food, little chap.
How often must I tell you
I haven't got a scrap?

'Probably your brother
I was chatting to.
In one way or another
He looks a bit like you.'
        . . . .
Hovering above, unheard:

Intruder! An attack!
My sparrow or brother bird,
A kestrel on its back.

'Sorry, little fellow;
No wisdom, little chap,
To tell for what befell you:
I haven't got a scrap.'

*

Gossamer web: its symmetry
Hung beauteous with morning dew.
But flies, who don't read poetry,
Have a different point of view.

*

Familiar view, upside down, framed by my legs
  –   As novel and as piquant as toast on eggs.

*

In future, squirrel, kindly learn
When feeding from me to discern
Between my finger and the nut.
Fingers bleed when sharply cut
By rodent teeth – and hospitals
Have even sharper pointed tools.
My reward for trying to be kind:
Twice rudely pierced – front and behind.

*

Sharp and long, the shadow places
Cast by pebbles and beech-nut cases
Made pebble paths where morning shone
Too startling to be trodden on.

*

A few loose leaves, a dying year,
An emptiness. What more?
I stop before a winter tree and stare
At twigs and branches interlaced
With sky – the leaves replaced
By patterned space and parent tree;
And worry in case someone might see,
Silhouetted against darkening sky,
Me… gazing at wood – and wonder why.

WALTHAMSTOW MARSH

Eastward the marshland soaking up the Lee,
Where wild willows kowtow to the pylon tree
And cow-parsley spreads like a bridal train
Over city debris – and it's spring again;
And you plod through mud, the city out of sight,
In a No-Man's-Land where the heron's flight,
The hovering kestrel, the Canada goose,
Bring, if not peace, a kind of truce.
The suburbs slug it out, but away from it all
The marsh resounds to the cuckoo's call,
And the suburbs forgotten crumble and fall.

But in summer when rushes spear a fen-like sky
And the sad days drag and the mud paths dry,
Wander in evening to a grassy railway track –
Liverpool Street Station a mile or two back –
On cracked thistle paths of hard-baked crust
Where things that grow hide things that rust,
Abandoned cars, and youthful lust,
And centipede trains with two feet in the air
Crawl forever to and fro to God knows where –
And you wonder if the marshland ever unlocks
To those who seek, its paradox.

Paradox? What paradox? Any fool can see –
Did they plant baby pylons? – there is no mystery.
Wildlife, people (flesh and blood right through)
Share land and water where things grow – and grew
Before man poked his nose in. Look again.
The town resurrected, what is there to explain?

But the marsh is softly burning: each pane
Of tower block glass ignited from the west.
A swan floats by with a gold leaf at its breast;
And the red-waved reservoir reminds you of the sea
A goose flight from the 253.

CHINESE GEESE

Too fat to fly, they know their place:
On top! – unlike the lower breeds they chase
Away: ducks and their ilk, who will intrude
When folk like me come armed with food.
Yet having satisfied inner-goose needs,
They act much like those lesser breeds:
Preen a bit, peck a bit, plod a bit, swim;
Squawk a bit, snooze a bit balanced on one limb;
Stretch a bit, scratch a bit, sit a bit, gaze
With stark weird eyes which see both ways;
Then a nap with no gap between tail and mouth,
Neck facing north, tummy settled south…
And you wonder at times whose world is true,
And what poem a goose would write of you.

Springtime brings – half fluff – half feet –
Little ones born chasing something to eat:
All rubber-stamped from beak to behind,
All of one body, all of one mind:
Flap a bit, scrap a bit, nap a bit – you know:
Guzzle, gargle, goggle; grow
       GROW,
         GROW.

Lords of the pond? Landed gentry let's say,
Following-my-leader the whole goose day –
Until, that is, there's food in sight,
Or a threat to be met (deprived of flight).
Then Follow Father's Footsteps? Superior air?
It's all fuss and feathers, and the first one there –

31

With outraged cries and outstretched necks,
Regardless of rank, or age, or sex.

CLOSE ENCOUNTERS IN THE TUBE

Rush hour. Crush hour. Squeeze in. Sway.
Try to read The Poem. Head in the way.
So stare deadpan into outer space,
Inches, worlds, from the next dead face.

Dead? The entire gamut of human themes
Is played out in tunnels: a thousand dreams
Change at Charing Cross, call at Baker Street
Via Babylon (faces stone discreet).
Next stop Heaven or (mind the gap) Hell?
Heads in the way; you just can't tell.

A stop. Edge along as pressure demands.
A man, portly, 30ish, looks up and stands
With a have-my-seat gesture; but instead
The young woman favoured shakes her head.

'Please!' Knight errant on the Bakerloo,
The lady won't play: she is younger than you.
Two wills harden. Two worlds collide –
Worlds apart – head on – dream denied
By an empty seat, locked in near embrace;
The rest of us resolutely lost in space.

THE WRITING ON THE WALL

Graffiti is Vandalism –
London Transport notice

'Sudden prayers make God jump'
Side by side with 'James woz ere'
Makes the point: you can't just lump
Graffiti together, any more than beer
Adverts – or verse, for that matter.
I, having more authorised escape avenues
For my brand of scribbled chatter,
Need no recourse to the walls of loos.
Others do. 'Children should be obscene
And not absurd' irritates no more
And harms less than its original, seen
For what it is. Vandalism? I'm not sure.

PLAYTIME

That slight frown as his records are scanned,
The curt if courteous questions, the roll play…
    But no, not this time; an outstretched hand,
Almost. A sherry? Sadly not, but 'By the way…'

By the way, by the side of the desk in fact,
Sits Unknown Youth, notebook poised, poker stiff,
Earnestly discreet – a model of textbook tact.
A student, if I don't mind. That solicitous 'If…'

Haemorrhoids you mind, infected toe no. Infected
Chest? Oh well. Shirt off, mouth open, closed:
Deep breathing and deep silent laughter undetected
By his stethoscope; misplaced mirth undiagnosed.

Do I smoke? (I, a teacher.) No, I don't smoke.
'Setting a good example, eh?' More smiles. I say
I never did – *smoke,* that is. A little joke.
Such bonhomie, we three. (We, not they.)

    Minding their own November morning business,
Figures pass by like Plato's shadows cast by fire
On cave walls. Unreal. Sentient, nonetheless.
Pain is real. And real enough the 'Hello Squire!

How are we today?' – the too-familiar eager cry
Of my neighbour inviting me to share with him
His sad lot, not mine. 'An X-ray? You? Why,
(Pawn to e4), you're a young man, Sunny Jim!'

Now, (bishop to b5), how old did I think he was?
–   And all on his own. I play safe, knock off
Six years then feign surprise, as one does,
Smile and withdraw. Must go; you know – a cough.

MURDER IN THE BANDSTAND

Tea 4.30, dinner at 7. A little stronger
each day. Bare toes reshaping the horizon…
a police band playing June out, July in…
the sun out and in. Toast and marmalade
in the morning, a balcony with bougainvillea
in the afternoon. The vocalist is good.
                              Somehow
you don't associate the Met with Sorrento –
                              songs like that.

Yesterday, Down Mexico Way (Acapulco without
diarrhoea) and Sussex-by-the-Sea (donkeys,
a deckchair for tuppence, and days that last
for ever); today, Annie Laurie and a final aria
to bring colour to the cheeks of the afternoon
–   with no premonition of foul play.
                              Somehow
you don't associate Eastbourne with murder –
                              things like that.

2 shots out of the blue. He falls clutching.
A sudden silence. Sounds of beach and traffic.
A siren. Unfolding laughter… and a top note
triumphant: not where it left off, but now
empowered with the authority of resurrection.
A cosy cathartic crisis to bond us.
                              Somehow
you don't expect the shared emotion. Tea –
                              4.30, dinner at 7.

37

GHOSTS

Oddly incongruous, the dark dank pier
Defies time, dripping atmosphere.
    The ghost train's gone.
             Real ghosts appear,
Strolling, laughing, hand in hand,
Past crumbling halls, a silent band,
A Grand Pavilion softly lit
In fairy lights where old ghosts sit,
Ghost lovers dance, ghost children play,
Dressed in clothes of yesterday.
    A sudden shriek from fun-ghost trains
Frightens real ghosts.
           One remains:
An old man with a ghost-child's eyes,
Startled by a seagull's cries.

ON KILLING

I sometimes wish
On summer days like this, the pier
Hurt only with the kind of pain sea and sky
Bring, without the sudden stab: a fish
Hauled choking silently through air,
To gape at gaping passers by.

I sometimes take
The harbour walk instead, yet know
Neither gulls nor rugged faces bent over net
Are bent on cosy pictures for my sake: –
Stalwart souls, soulful birds, owe
Like me a debt to death; yet

I sometimes think
If all pain showed itself in cries,
All fear, some things I kill I would not kill.
But silent terror serves to blur the link
Between what dies and what else dies
Each time a thing lies still.

VOYAGE

Jet travel is a form of cheating:
Going direct to the answer book
Instead of grappling with the questions.

Their hair and the port receding,
They stand waving to empty spaces on the quayside;
Bedecked by broken streamers, they turn to empty places
On pleasure decks… outstretched on their shadows.
For what is new under the sun:
Decks bedecked by breasts that hide their secrets?

The ship is full of strangers
Who are kindly requested to call at the purser's office
To collect a telegram, a teddy bear, a lost child,
A lost youth… The bars are full of men of laughter.
Playing cards, they missed
The porpoises. Drinking beer, they missed the port.

*

'Rough, you say? Call this rough?
    Here's to the Bay of Biscay!
One more drink? You've had enough?
    I'll have another whisky.

'The Red Sea now… there last June.
    Red Sea? – more, blue jelly.
The nights. Magic. Big full moon.
    You can't get that on telly.

40

'I used to chase the sun. Too hot.
    Went north. Too damned cold.
Always wanted what I hadn't got –
    And now I'm getting old.

'Sea. Life. Same, so to speak…
    See that chap? Chief Engineer.
He says the ship's *supposed* to creak!
    Steady! You need a beer.

'Life! – a mad dentist. Raves, rants,
    But his chair is soft beneath.
You can choose to live in shiny pants,
    Or die without your teeth.'

                    *

A lesson on board – and I
Eavesdropping at the next table
Could never resist a lesson.
Just a sweet child, her tutor – and me.
Who knows what we shall learn?
    But what is this?
We have to find the adjectival clause.
Why, Madam, the adjectival clause?
What can we do with it if we find it?
We cannot play with it or eat it.
It does not squeak when you press it.
It will not comfort you at night.
You cannot stroke it.
You cannot even put it in a poem –
At least I do not know how
And it's too late to start now.
    Look! Over there a sun of sorts

Begins to play with banks of clouds
And breaks the harmony that holds
The morning. And, see, flying fish
In tight-lipped seas, defying
A kind of ordained tranquillity.
  Why, Madam,
Do we need an adjectival clause?

When you have found it, child,
Show it to me that I may know it.
I will draw funny arms and legs to it,
Rolling eyes, a big moustache,
And we will give it a nicer name
And keep it safe forever –
Just the two of us, you and me.
It will be our secret.

*

Exuding sex
And lovesick charm,
They pace the decks
Locked arm in arm,
In T-shirts, shorts –
All chest and thigh,
Whispering thoughts…
So deep her sigh.
How come she sports
A fresh black eye?

*

At what sublime moment summer became
Winter the sea, indifferent, gave no sign:
(Amber lights? An island?). All the same,

A diffused numinous calm, hard to define,
Made standing on one's shadow's head
Whispering to God things He already knew,
Seem mystical. Someone (not God) said,
'Neptune's coming!' – with half the crew
His court or prisoners, judging by the din.
   Beside the pool, squashed with the rest,
I watched men throw each other in
(Tarzan cries, faces painted, fully dressed),
And later, sitting where Neptune had sat,
Recalled those words of Wittgenstein:
'It is not *how* **things are… but** *that***…'**
That there's anything:
                    this white speck in sparkling wine
Floating where the world divides; high jinks
For the customers; shadow lost; Tarzan's call;
Knowing where to turn if the ship sinks;
Getting drunk; drowning… The Mystical.

                    *

   A metal door
   Gripped too tight
   Divides the dancers
   From the night,
   Separates pretty
   From pristine light.
   Terror! Terror!
   Burning bright –
   The stars… spears!
   Blake was right.

                    *

43

Descending from the empty balcony of morning,
Stretched out wide across the white gangway
Ships put down, asserting their right of way,
The albatross glides – glacial, silent, aloof,
And hangs suspended between the shaking floor
    and roof.
We are the sole spectators. We are the Play.
No plot. No denouement. Day follows day.

Left to itself the southern ocean sulks, frets,
Flicks spray into winter sunlight, making rainbows.
    We rock on rainbows.
Teased all day, the ocean rises… high on rainbows;
Tosses its loose change at the face of the sky,
Swallows rainbows whole like water, calls for more:
    Double rainbows;
Spits out pieces against the walls of the sky;
Waves to the sky. A cosmic celebration.

In fading light sea and sky cavort together,
Plunging forward, lurching sideways: sea to port,
    Sky to starboard:
Walls of water curling, calling, rising, falling,
As we stand watching, retching, praying… paddling
In slippered feet where sea and cabin carpets meet,
    Intruders at the party.
A gate-crashing wave with plate-smashing spite
Confirms that dinner will be delayed tonight.

              *

    The albatross which stretched out
    Each morning on a stage-lit sea,

Lunched with us, stayed to tea –
Graciously content to hang about
By lonely ships (though more at ease
With pastures lonelier than these)
Until he sensed the unseen shore
Where blind men rule so can't be for
Kings who reign by rainbow seas.

And if they question me, the blind:
Do I carry precious things:
Jewels, perfumes, diamond rings…?
If they search, what can they find? –
The groping blind men waiting there
Who walk on land (but I on air).

I hid from them the Southern Cross,
The sea, the clouds, an albatross –
Gifts too special to declare.

BOYS ONCE

Growing up between wars
Meant growing up with Empire, King and Country,
And – joining us each November in a bleak extended
Assembly – The Dead who died for us and Freedom.
Freedom! this from a breed of wiry whackers
(Now extinct) who would 'deal with you, my boy' for
Calculated acts of valour like whispering in class,
Whistling in line, or turning Left when the command
Was Right. As for Them, the Resolute and Glorious,
Immortalised in marble, we never thought of them
As boys once, normal, noisy, pimply, picked on: us
One generation less lucky.

Grown up one war later –
The path from adolescence to manhood entrusted to
The care of poker-backed NCOs – we heard of others:
Brave men who would never grow old, their duty done.
Duty! – the word resonates uneasily still: echoes
Of early cruelty coated in piety. Who were they,
These lads who fell whistling in face of the foe,
Turning neither left nor right? Real, not marble,
The big boys in the playground lines, regulation
Caps jauntily awry. I don't blame those old-time
Schoolmasters for any bitter endings… only for
Less-than-sweet beginnings.

BIG MAN GETTING ME DOWN
(Circa 1943)

'Mannerisms, my lad,' the liftman said.
'What you need to learn is good mannerisms.'

You could hardly blame him, poor cuss:
Ascending, descending… responding to a bell
9 to 5 like a Pavlovian dog. Forty plus.
Fixed frown. Chest ribbons on display.
A different uniform these days, a lesser hell,
But at the beck and call of all comers:
A kind of death in its way.
And here's this whippersnapper of 16 summers
Too bloody lazy to take a flight of stairs
(Well, 5 or 6). Expect him to ooze charm? –
Up, down… Up, down… All day.

Yet there were others you met with no air
Of You'd-better-watch-it-my-lad. No airs
At all. Sometimes no eye – no leg – no arm;
In pairs with a barrel organ. Pride masked,
But cloth caps their begging bowls; their lot
Sadder than his. And all of them once basked
In glory: *UP!… Over the top! DOWN!… Get down!*
So you make allowances. Or maybe not.
Maybe he's no hero, just a puffed-up gnat
Taking it out on a kid. I could have asked
Him, but good manners precluded that.

OLD SOLDIERS ALWAYS DIE

When the ship went down
He obediently took his turn
At the end of the queue.
If someone has to drown,
They taught him, or burn,
Better he than I or you.

Rising 60 now and no sign
Of a bus pass, his sour half-
Guilty thoughts persist:
Ahead in the wrong line
Now, a first and last laugh
Both somehow missed.

DREAMS WITHIN A DREAM

Almost comical, almost conical, the old dears board
buses to date younger men in white coats – *Hold tight
ladies!* – their poor feet killing them. Dying, who needs
    seats…?

And the slim girls in fitted costumes and stiletto heels,
 clutching shiny handbags, smile up with red-lipped
 smiles at young men not yet dead, in dead blacked-out
    streets…

And the children, paired in narrow desks, sit in silence,
dipping steel nibs into stained inkpots, as rule-bound as
the po-faced clock – and too young to know Time
    cheats…

'**I...**'

I... 'that old woman' hobbling by,
Weary of limb, with drooping eye –
I am the child with the skipping rope,
My world a song whose theme is Hope.
Yes, I the cripple crawl past where
A schoolgirl runs with windswept hair;
And I am the toddler, face all jam,
In high-heel shoes: not was, *am;*
I am the baby in the pram –
Precious, adored: my parents' pride;
I am their dream. And I am the bride,
Flowers in my hand, silk at my feet,
Love in my eyes: the circle complete –
I am the point at which all lines meet.
I who am lonely, grey, a bore,
Am the fun-girl young men don't ignore,
The widow whose first husband dies
In wartime when the whole world cries;
In middle age I know death, pain,
Joy and wonder, death again;
I see time laugh, I see time weep;
I am the years that fell asleep
And woke to find a time to keep...
They can no longer pass me by:
I am them all, and they are I.

FIRST KISS

On a day like this we met
Underneath abandoned trees.
No point you said in getting wet;
Stay, soon the storm will ease.

So I waited, softly praying
For the rain to set well in;
Drank in all that you were saying,
Raindrops dripping down my chin.

Lovely when you smiled at me,
Sandals soggy, hair a wreck.
Simply that you smiled at me –
Blobs of water down my neck.

Underneath the trees you kissed
Me, on a day like this.
Thunderbolts? If so they missed
Me, deflected by your kiss.

ULTIMATE QUESTIONS

In his teens he reached out to Heaven,
Found nothing to hold on to and toppled.
Shaken up, he set out to gun down
The god he had been taught to love,
Convinced the affair was not mutual.
His aim was poor, his vision limited.

God survived.

You don't get away with things like
That! and no questions asked. Still
Helping with inquiries, a showdown looming,
He can't decide whether to throw himself
Abjectly at the mercy of the Court
Or refuse to recognise its authority.

HEATWAVE

Dollis Brook, August 2003

Patterns of light and shade
imprinted on path and foliage,
the body sticky, the stillness
palpitating – any movement,
any sound, a violation of some primeval
overarching inviolable Order.

We bought a large voluptuous melon
for a few annas by the dried-up mudbanks
where turtles fed, and, thirst satisfied,
left it there, too cumbersome to carry.
A drenching walk back just the same.
Still no rain,
Only the intermittent sound of thunder.

A drenching walk back… ripe
blackberries in the hedgerows;
trembling trees growing down
to meet sky in still water.
The first hint of thunder.
No sign of a tonga, let alone a 240.

In August 2003 the shade temperature in London
reached 100 degrees F, the highest ever recorded.

CORPORAL SAHIB
1947

After the wilderness – the manna rationed –
We woke white-faced in a Land not Promised:
Boy soldiers dressed to kill with nowhere to go;
                                        Sahibs
In a land where no Sahib cleans his own shoes.
Men without shoes, saluting, told us so.
    We the uninvited… the unconsulted.

    And it was evening.

Long-sleeved evenings alive with whispers.
Under each naked lamp grotesque silent casts
Perform their frenzied dances, ignored.

Beer! Double eggs and chips! Poetry and song.
        16 annas one rupee,
        17 annas one buckshee
        O doolally sahib, O doolally sahib…
Over-polite, perspiring, liveried bearers smile
Their fixed shy smiles. More beer, Johnny! Beer
And *O'Riley's Daughter:* an Anthem. Sod the heat,
The prickly heat, the routine void that was today,
The ordained emptiness that will be tomorrow!
Sing of the daughter of the one-eyed Riley! Sing
Songs to silence whispers…
        O doolally sahib, O doolally sahib,
        May the boat that takes you home
        Ditch you in the parni, sahib.

                                          Nights of the Raj:
Chips in the canteen, chapatis on the verandah,
Forster in the library, the stars in their places.
We all in the same boat – with nobody's daughter.

   And it was morning.

Rigid in ranks, the bespectacled blind stand
In avenues of their shadows, forbidden to wriggle,
Rivulets of sweat dammed halfway by elastic.
        "STAND STILL, CORPORAL!"
Answer him. Politely. "Don't mind me, sir,
But spare a thought for the coolies and sweepers
Glancing pursed-lipped at their pocket watches.
These people don't like to be kept waiting, sir."

                                    Armies of black ants
In unbroken lines traverse the cracked parched soil.
Kites with unprotected eyes patrol unbroken skies.

                              In a sombre workshed
We, Mr Khan, Mr Pant and the punkah wallah etiolate
– Equal each in the light of Ultimate Reality.

                           Forms completed in duplicate;
Forster, in duplicity. Simla, Peshawar, Rawalpindi,
Are stencilled names on wooden packing crates.

   Lahore, our ultimate reality.

Tiffin and a tumbler of salt water. Your health!

And yet a little sleep, a little slumber…naked
But for a hand towel, the flies immune to curses.
A tree rat in…and out. A flying beetle in…
And out for ever.
                    Yesterday (or perhaps it was today)
The white empty afternoon, left to burn itself out,
Drifted lost into lost summer days when summer
Was childhood, sunlit and softly shadowed.
                    Today (or perhaps it was yesterday)
The Ganges flows through the hair of Shiva
And parallel lines meet in infinity and infinity
Is India at sunset when the pillars of cumulus
Holding up the sky break into myriads of islands
Floating crimson-edged in a green translucent sea;
And before the day reawakens to cards and camaraderie,
To sweet tea, green oranges and dog-eared paperbacks,
Time locked in incredulity has time to hold its breath:
That this is. That this is now.
                    This. Now. (Or perhaps it was never.)

    Twice weekly the gharris take us to Lahore:
Not the Mughal city hiding behind walls; nor
The Gardens of Shalimar, whose fountains they say
Refresh the air and the soul. The Museum? –
Why not the Museum? – the ivory made flesh:
Each warrior pawn unique, precious…priceless…
Created by Man in his own image.
                    Paradise enow:
Iced coffee. Sandwiches with the crusts removed.
Cinemas with real seats. Horse-drawn tongas
With tinkling bells and mellow evening lamps –
A romantic evocation of romance deferred.
                    Young man-about-town,

Your silk shirt hand-made by the Camp tailor,
Your stylish rakish topee purchased in Bombay,
You will be very lucky. Three girls love you.
The man in the red turban said so. Fate
Has tossed its coin and called. For a small fee
The man in the red turban will reveal more...

                      And they in their tongas,
The ladies in purdah and the ladies in fine saris,
Impassive in streets with impeccable English names,
They too will be lucky? And those who sleep at night
Supine on railway platforms – they too?

                      I am left with a picture.
A castle with pointed turrets: the railway station
Disguised. Upturned palms pressed together. *Salaam.*
A hissed whisper: "Shake hands! Shake hands!" –
The picture moving, the last frame shaking.

PART TWO

SCHOOL – Scenes from a changing world

MORNING ASSEMBLY

'The school day… shall begin with collective worship…'
                                        Education Act.

'Sir! Miss! Flo has had pups!'
The staff were enjoying a quiet tea and chat
Until the morning invasion altered all that.
Door flung open. Clatter of cups.
In the face of each messenger there to be seen
What the staff had forgotten: what miracles mean.
'Sir! Miss! Flo has had pups!'

'Puppies! C'mon… in the shed!'
It was almost as if they stood worshipping there,
Eyes kindled with awe. No hymns; no prayer;
Just wonder – sheer wonder – instead:
The children, staff, parents, and the lollipop man,
Cooks, cleaners, caretaker… A bright girl ran –
Bless her! – to wake up the Head.

'Sir, sir, you'll never guess what!'
Guessing games, oh dear, not at this time of day.
Phone calls and forms… still, he'd better play.
'Don't tell me. Am I warm… hot?'
'No, no, sir, its Flo, sir…' He found them all
Silent, assembled… bright-eyed at the miracle.
Dear Sir Harry,
        You'll never guess what…

'E-mails, letters… most tommyrot.'
The Chief Inspector paused. 'What's this? Hello!

Three wriggling little 'uns just born to old Flo?
Meetings. Damn! I'll say I forgot.'
If only more schools gave him good news like this.
An inspector inspects; he'd be damned if he'd miss
Seeing Old Sad Eyes rocking her cot.

'A school dog. Pups. What on earth!'
No wonder the Private Secretary seemed distraught.
What on earth should he do with Sir Harry's report?
Shred it? More than his job was worth.
He blew his nose, stood up and crossed the floor,
Breathed in deeply, then tapped on a Special Door.
'A miracle, Ma'am, a time of birth.'

Mother and babies well. Well, well!
People told people. The good news brought cheer
In workplace and cottage… over tea, over beer.
Output rose. The crime rate fell.
Three 'bundles of happiness', as The Broadcast said,
Causing ripples of joy; and the ripples still spread,
To end – where? No one can tell.

But suppose – *suppose* – 'Flo: pups 3'
Was recorded in flame by a white figure with wings
In that part of heaven which deals with these things.
What if he watches, what does he see?
The children, staff, parents, and the lollipop man,
Cooks, cleaners, and caretaker (Flo's greatest fan),
The Chief Inspector and wife (both spick and span)
With the driver and mates from the School Meals van,
Some Governors, the postman, and Fred Appleboy's gran
… All wide-eyed, side by side, where new life began
– A miraculous morning assembly.

LULLABY

Sailor-suit boy
with the Jubilee mug,
tidy up your soldiers,
say your little prayer,
clean your teeth, kiss
daddy, granny – Oh look,
an airship – a zeppelin –
golden in the evening air.

Sweet dreams, sailor.
Mummy loves you,
the king loves you,
everyone loves everyone.
How sweetly the king smiled
at the cheering children
waving little flags,
thirsty in the hot sun.

School is sandcastles,
Oranges and Lemons,
Right turn, Left turn,
Attention, STAND STILL!
How sweetly the teachers smile
at the waiting mothers
who know nothing ever does,
or ever will.

Little boys grow up
brave like their daddies
who once fought grey dragons,

fierce, fiery and strong.
Softly the night spreads,
softly the stars laugh…
Sleep, Bubbles, sleep,
the night is long.

RISING SIX

'Child, don't shout! –
If you don't understand
Do not call out.
Put up your hand.'

So I went everywhere
With rules to keep;
One hand in the air,
Calling out in my sleep.

YOU SPOKE

'Come out! Stand there –
I shall deal with you soon.'

You spoke. *Spoke!* Bear
Witness ye earth, sun, moon.

YOU ARE A BOY

You are a boy, therefore you will be beaten
Sooner or later; probably sooner, then later.
There is no need for you to behave badly or
Stupidly. You are a boy. That is sufficient.

The beater has your welfare at heart. Cooperate
With him. Do not bring disgrace on yourself,
Your class, your school, your gender, by crying;
Certainly not in the presence of your peers.
Lavatories (usually) have locks on their doors.

It always helps to retain a sense of humour.
Here your benefactor may be of assistance.
Some masters have set jokes for the occasion.
The quick-witted may even improvise – although
This cannot be guaranteed if they are angry.
Some masters hit only if angry or provoked!
One must allow for the vagaries of human nature.

Never fall into the common trap of supposing
All beaters enjoy beating. Some do, obviously;
Others less obviously. But does this matter?
Look ahead. Think of the many chortling years
Of reminiscing with like-minded friends – *proof*
That it never did you – or them – any harm.

A word of caution. Try not to acquire a taste
For the experience. Regrettably this can happen.
In school the service is free, and sanctioned.
In later life such predilections involve expense

And embarrassment. But then you are only 7.
Time enough to worry about these things.
Run along now.

MEET THE CLASS

Now here is Sally,
well known to herself as Sally
–   as in 'Well done, Sally!'
rarely as Sally Jones
–   as in 'Really, Sally Jones,
I am surprised at *you*!'
No one is surprised by Sally.
    And here is the GP,
mother of two, early feminist
campaigner for worthy causes
and competent cellist.
    And here is the dead girl,
stabbed by her lover. A pair
of household scissors, they say.
The full story will never be known.

Now here is Jones,
too old these days for Ronald
so called Jones (what else?):
Jones when he's thoughtful,
Jones when he's silly:
'You're a fool, Jones! What
are you?' 'A fool, Sir.'
    And here is the soldier
who wants to be a vicar,
playing Beethoven quartets
on a wind-up gramophone.

And here is the quiet boy
diagnosed at thirty, his
first novel half-finished.
The full story will never be known.

Now here are the others,
sitting arms folded: 40 faces,
40 labels, 40 stories unknown –
policeman, artist, typist,
salesman, fraudster, victim…
This week's composition is
What I Should Like To Be
For A Day – everything possible.
So fly away Maureen, Susan, Tammy,
Chatterbox Jane, Ginger Allen,
Brainy Brenner, Late-again Truman…
For one hour until playtime,
a princess, a pony, a wild bird,
a clown, a ghost, a magic carpet,
God, a shiny new penny…

WHO DO YOU STICK UP FOR, SIR?

The crucial division in the school
        is not between boys and sirs,
But between those who worship Arsenal
        and those who pray for Spurs.

TEACHER ON PLAYGROUND DUTY

Being tall, he could not see
The *Queen Mary* racing the *Normandie*,
Only – following the fall of rain –
2 matchsticks floating to the drain.

MORNING ARITHMETIC

Rows of sums… You sit in rows,
Wrinkles on your brow, ink all on your nose.
Your left hand's curled to make a screen
Round work too sacred to be seen.
You're not allowed to copy, cheat,
Count on your fingers, count on your feet,
Whisper, fidget, chatter, chew,
Budge from your seat, go to the loo,
Write on your blotter, make a blot –
'Sir, can I –?' No, you may NOT!
It's worse than that. You mustn't weep,
Scream, break down, fall asleep,
Take off your jacket; take off your tie,
Take off your shirt… make love… die!
Just page after page of filthy sums,
And hours to go till playtime comes.
But cheer up, children. Life is kind.
That's the fire alarm! Time to unwind.

HEAD BOY

At Play

Held high – high in self-esteem –
The head of the Head Boy in the team
Will toss a condescending nod
Occasionally these days to God.

Ungrateful Heaven, for its part,
Saves most applause for some upstart
Who regards each ball as fun;
And makes a hit with every one.

HEAD BOY

On Duty

I did not say 'personal autonomy':
I said 'Persons-ought-to-honour-me'.

TIME, YOU THIEF

Remember Alec? Everyone's pal,
But tough! – he trained with weights.
You'd go up to him with your mates
And say, 'Show us your muscles, Al.'
He'd grin, roll his sleeves, display
Charles Atlas biceps. You'd say,
All pop-eyed, 'Let's have a feel.'
Mr Universe! Flesh like steel.

He came back today. What hits
You first is the change: face
Thinner, nose longer; you can't place
What's wrong. Nothing fits.
He is… and he isn't. No grin.
No Chest out, Ally-boy, tummy in!
A stranger with a flash tie
Managed a wink, and passed by.

STUDENT-TEACHER

Intermittent SHUT UPs thunder across the Hall
from areas of conflict, drawing retaliatory fire.
Ideals topple. Cherished beliefs lie fragmented…
the sniggering girls no better than the sniping boys.

Children, for goodness sake! A school, just a school:
Rules, rituals, traditions, big beasts, little beasts,
Keep to the Paths… Do Not Climb the Trees –
Go to sleep! Madness, this language of battle.

Only children. Real soldiers cost 6d at Woolworths.
Red sails are in the sunset. *Sleep… sleep…*
Mummy and Charles Boyer are in the Garden of Allah.
Coloured fairy lights hang on seaside trees.

SWEET JENNIFER

Sweet Jennifer – always top!
No wonder. Work? – she doesn't stop.
Busy like a bee; it makes you sick.
Enjoys spelling tests! Arithmetic? –
Gobbles up problems, asks for more,
And helps Miss out if *she's* not sure.
Guess whose needlework's on display!
Guess who recited last Prize Day!
You know the type: never fails
To practise her piano scales;
Handwriting disgustingly neat;
Good at team games, doesn't cheat;
And always 'keeps herself amused';
And never asks to 'be excused'…
In short, a crawling, smug, appalling
                              BRAT!?
Well no, she's not a bit like that.
She's sweet, unspoilt, simply la crème.

You wonder what becomes of them.

STILL SWEET JENNIFER

Young Jenny Jay, B.Mus., B.Ed.,
Smiles a lot, calls children 'dear' –
(Even those who aren't) – and instead
Of 'Sit up!…Sing up!... I can't hear
You!… There is no need to shout.',
Says, 'You sing like angels.' Maybe so,
Though with so few of those about,
Ask yourself, how does she know?

Sometimes at night Ms Jay flat out
Wonders if it's all worth while.
But Tom has forgotten again to clout
Some kid, basking still in JJ's smile.
Poor Ann's asleep, strangely content.
In her mad dream school bells ring;
Nothing means what once it meant,
But Ms Jay smiles – and angels sing.

MAY QUEEN

… So they give out this slip, right?
and say it's a secret ballot, don't sign,
it's called Democracy. All you do is write
the name of one girl. I wrote mine,
but everybody knew it was between
Linda and Beverley, and – more's the pity –
Linda won. You want to be a May Queen?
Rule 1 (there's no Rule 2): Be pretty!
Dead easy. It tells you how in the mags.
Eat fresh fruit and broccoli, stuff
like that, right? and keep off the fags.
Short and fat? Gawky with glasses? Tough!
You think some people get too much – a lot
too much – attention as it is? Who cares?
Go home, look in the mirror, hatch a plot
to murder Linda, say your prayers,
then lie awake staring at the night.
A queen?
Who doesn't dream at times? Right?

THE TRUTH

'Sir,' said Janet,
'Pat called me a pig.'
It mattered:
Eyes hurt and big,
Cheeks fired.
'And are you a pig?' –
Gravely enquired.
'No, sir,' said Janet
(A truthful child).
'What are you then?'
   –   And Janet smiled.
'A little girl.'…
And suddenly shy.

Poor Pat, caught out:
And such a whopping lie!

NOT YOU AGAIN

If Attila… Genghis Khan… Napoleon… Adolf Hitler…
Had done all their fighting when they were littler,
The world would have been spared its worst disasters.

Someone please explain this to all headmasters.

'COME IN!'

The Headmaster's Story

    'It's this kid, see.
    He keeps on startin' on me,
    An' jus' because I touched 'im on the 'ead
    Miss said I gotta see you… Miss said.'

That's the reluctant tap. There's the confident one,
The *rat-tat* that makes you reach for your gun.
No word has been spoken, the door's unopened yet,
But just as the sounds of a string quartet
Differ from the drama of rock band drums,
So the taps of the timid from the raps of irate mums.

    'You the headmaster? See this shirt?
    Look at it. Covered with dirt.
    Torn! – Hardly worn. A blooming disgrace!
    I want to know what's going on in this place.
    It was his trousers last time –
    Yes, I keep telling him not to climb…'

Some knocks bring foreboding. Whither fate?
You pause, call 'Come in', you wonder, you wait.
A door is like an instrument **everyone plays**
According to mood and message: knocks are give-
aways;
Preludes to action; duets for voice and wood –
With a player on each side. Seldom understood.
                                        'COME IN!'

'Excuse me, Miss – I mean Sir,
2 things, well 3 really. Miss wants to lend
The globe and she says are you coming to play
For the choir because if not, she said to say,
What with the workmen her nerves'll break –
And I brought you a piece of my birthday cake.'

THE CHOICE

An excuse was found to send both boys
out of the room; the rest of us called together,
in confidence, he said. (One of those ploys
to grab instant attention?) Problem: whether
to award the art prize to Sidney or to John,
both outstanding, as we knew. For his part,
he'd prefer no prizes. Not two? Better none.
Goals are scored in football – not art.

Some things you can measure. Art is something
else. So? Consulted, we voted. A duty done.
A solemn choice between the colours of spring
and the colours of autumn. And Sidney won.
And in a way we all did, though not because
it would have seemed so wrong had it gone
the other way. Someone said after the pause,
'Let's club together to buy a gift for John.'

PRIZE DAY

Flowers
Everywhere around the hall,
Like at a wedding
Or a funeral.
Visitors
Who smile that Special Smile
Kids sometimes use when things go wrong:
It's much too wide,
It goes on too long.
Bouquets too in what they say,
Unlike the rehearsals
Yesterday.

Flowers:
A posy for each lady guest.
The headmaster,
Backbone and trousers pressed,
Finds his glasses:
The school is blessed.
4B recites,
The choir sings,
The visitors hear of wonderful things:
A new toilet block,
The 11-plus test,
The netball team's triumph against all odds,
The Game of Life played without cheating.
The guests grow sterner,
The Mayor sounds impressed.
She says she thinks
The children of this school need some beating.

A teacher winks.
The headmaster nods.
At the back someone giggles.
A finger
Prods.

Eyes
Study the Mayor.
She wears a Dick Turpin hat,
A red gown whiskered with fur.
She's called *His* Worship
Instead of *Her.*
(Mr Cannon's black gown also causes a stir.
He's called Big Bertha
As well as –
Sir.)

Hands
Outstretched too soon,
Like a baby's mouth open wide for the spoon.
Hands that give,
Hands that take,
Hands that clap,
Hands that shake.
You take with the left,
Shake with the right.
Not always easy with everyone there.
Some hands confused
Jab the air.
A quick left and right
Land on the Mayor.
But she smiles, laughs, understands.
A Mayor's main job is shaking
Hands.

The recorders
Cross the sea to Skye.
The choir
Won't let Trelawney die.
Time for The Message!
(Who could have guessed?)
'We-can't-all-win-prizes-
But-we-can-all-do-our-best.'
And... A HOLIDAY tomorrow!
First ritual cheer.
Big Bertha puts hand to ear.
'I can't hear you.'
Broad smiles grow broader.
'I still can't hear you...'
Breakdown of order.
The mace-bearer rises,
Teeth and mace gleaming;
The Procession is led
Past children screaming,
Waking the dead;
Visitors beaming:
Sherry ahead.

Home, happy winners, clutching cricket bats,
Big books, *Little Women,* chemistry sets;
Home to more praise – to kisses and hugs.
And the others, the losers, to silence, shrugs?
Jealous? Resigned? No feelings at all?

Look back. What's left? An empty hall.
A well-polished floor. A few petals fall.

ORDER OF MERIT

'Finally, the prize for Disobedience
is awarded this year to... Florence.
Born, I see, in Florence, Florence –
1824. Ah, well! – foreign influence
and a wilful nature. But no excuse
for disobedience. Girls of your class
are expected to make exemplary use
of your talents, be attractive, and pass
the time demurely until ready to marry
the right Lord Tom, Colonel Dick,
or the right Right Reverend Doctor Harry;
not be obsessed with nursing the sick.
Heed this, girls. Give Florence a clap
but remember, Always Do As You Are Told.
And one day marry some brave young army chap
with whom you may grow gracefully old.'

TODAY'S GIRLS

What are today's girls coming to? Discussing her career,
Ruth says she wants to be a nurse and not an engineer!
But then she's only 12 today. Give her another year.

But Rachel's really quite grown up; few grow up faster.
She wants to be a teacher and marry the headmaster.
But then she's only 7 and I don't suppose he's asked her.

SEX EDUCATION

Jonathan kissed Joanne, you know,
Both washing up the painting dishes,
While the others watched that video
About the bees and birds and fishes
To which neither Jon nor Jo could go –
It was against their parents' wishes.

UNEQUAL COMBAT

Tell me, dear boy, how many teachers have you gunned down so far this morning?

—   Only a few, sir.

Reassuring. We both know one you wouldn't harm…

—   Who, sir?

Me. We're too fond of each other, which is why I seat you in front so close to me.

—   True, very true, sir.

So could you oblige me just this once and stop poking the boy behind you…

—   He did it too, sir.

… and get on with your diary. Isn't there anything you'd like to write about?

—   I haven't a clue, sir.

Well, those nature pictures at the back. Do you like them?

—   At least they're new, sir.

Then write about *them*. Describe them. What do they

say to you? Give me a surprise. Excite me.

— Coo, sir.

And when you've finished you may read your diary to
the class if you wish.

— Ready! Hello, folk. Here is my diary, and listen
  carefully. I have some exciting news. This
  morning we all had a big surprise. The pictures
  on the classroom wall have been... wait for it...
  CHANGED! We now have pictures of British
  wildlife at the back. Woof, woof...grrrr...grrrr...
  g-r-r-ro-w-l...a-o-o-o-u-u-u-gh... Will that do, sir?

And one dangerous live specimen in the front.

— Everybody's looking at you, sir.

INTRUDER

Earlier today a wasp flew
In through the classroom window.
  Although it never knew
Of rules – human or divine – like
  Thou shalt not kill,
It showed no concern, just a busy
  Sense of purpose. Still,
Neither would it have understood
  Thou shalt not sting –
Which served to concentrate minds,
  But not on the thing
Timetabled… a problem solved
  By a rolled-up magazine
And a swift blow, later justified:
  Someone might have been
Stung. Death also had its sting,
  Sharp enough to evoke
An unexpected sense of discomfort.
  For a time no one spoke.

CLASS PROJECT

Suspended from the ceiling
In outer classroom space,
A 2-scaled solar system:
Planets put in place

Not, as in the Bible,
By fourth day divine command,
But by human mathematics
And bruised and bleeding hand.

Children, they created
The children of the sun;
The planets shed their secrets
To them, one by one.

Jupiter, the red-eyed giant,
Saturn, a queen with rings,
Started life as chicken wire,
Canvas, other things.

Mercury? A marble once –
(A confiscated one?) –
Too hot now to handle,
Glared at by the sun.

How many miles to Pluto?
10-score to the power of 10?
Can we get there by speed of light?
One day, and back again.

Children drinking morning milk
Between Venus and Mars,
Travelling in the Milky Way
With 200 billion stars.

TEENAGE CONCEPTION

A first live poem struggling to be born.
These things happen: a school encounter, a seed
sown; and it's curtains for cute cuddly rhymes
and jokey jingles – though who doesn't need
to be tucked up and tickled at times?

The delivery is difficult. Nascent verse
has a will of its own. Words savoured, saved,
won't play together: bully-words hijack the game.
The newly-born need not be too well behaved,
but it must be yours just the same.

And yours it is, but sadly it is not *you*.
Such hard labour – and no smile, no song.
You can't show it off. Polite eyes will glaze,
smiles freeze; pauses will be too long.

Still inside you a real poem kicks and plays.

TOO LATE

'The saddest three words in the English language:
"It's too late."'
Thus spake Miss Zarathustra at assemblies, adding
'It's *never* too late.'

What this time? you wondered. 'A' levels taken or
A first parachute jump
By someone's granny? Either way, the same lesson:
It's *never* too late.

Sadly, there are sadder words in every language –
Au revoir les enfants
Among the saddest. By the time you understand why,
It's always too late.

MARY

Classroom with roses. 9, she chose
To pay this tribute to the rose:

> In June and July so lovely, gay.
> Why so soon to fade away…?

Roses dying. End of term evoked:
Autographs. Tears. Feeling choked.

An August beach. Paper half-read.
A back page item: *Crash girl dead.*

9 rose seasons. Still there to see,
In her own hand, her obituary:

> In June and July so lovely, gay
> Why so soon to fade away…?

SHEPHERD LOST

You grow too fond of them, the little lambs;
Then they go their own way on paths you shape
    but cannot share.
Who are these women wheeling their prams…
And the stranger who insists on paying your fare?

THE HIT

On Parents' Day
The old Punishment Book went on display.
Of all items it
Made without much doubt the biggest hit.
Who'd have believed –
Those who punished, those who received? –
This record of pain
Was entered, in the end, to entertain.

ODD MAN OUT

Poor Mrs Pringle's poorly,
The poor soul's far from well,
And Poor Sol is asked to take her class
An hour before the bell.
(Before the final bell, that is;
There's no break between each round.)
Sol strides in looking fierce,
Says he doesn't want a sound.
No sound from 1P? That's a laugh;
No one's the least bit scared.
Poor Sol, he hasn't got a hope –
And not a thing prepared.
One whole hour. What do you do
With the babbling little brutes? –
Jack and the Beanstalk? Jack the Ripper?
Pythagoras? Square roots?
A game. That's it, play a game…
Let them find the Odd Man Out.
Of course they'll have no paper, pens,
No pencil points, no doubt.
Still, shove some words up on the board,
They can find which ones don't fit.
'Right! SHUT UP! Give these out –
Don't comb her hair now. Everybody SIT!
He took your chair? That's your chair,
That's hers, you came in late.
Yes, you can draw a margin, dear.
No, you needn't put the date.'
Words… which words? Think fast, Sol.
Let's see… *Man… child… school…cat* –

They'll do. Dammit, what's the answer?
Keep 'em busy, that.
A cry. 'Got it! Yeah.' – from Daniel,
Naughty, but not a fool.
Will he say that *cat, man, child,*
All breathe: the odd one out is *school*?
Or see that *school, man, child,*
Are linked to humankind?
Human? Little brutes, thinks Sol.
Only kidding, kiddies… Never mind.
Danny's dancing in his seat, bursting to explain.
'Cat is the odd man out,' says Dan:
To him the reason's plain.
'Because a cat's got whiskers,
But a school, a child, a man,
Hasn't got no whiskers.' –
Now beat that if you can!

Poor Sol, his sudden laugh's cut short,
He sees the lad go red.
Remember what it's like to blush
For something that you said?
The little chap's got feelings. My!
Life is one big surprise.
A hundred fat books teach you less
Than the pain in one child's eyes.
Still, cheer up Sol, says Sol to Sol,
The world, as Dan points out,
Is full of cats with whiskers,
And full of schools without.
And full of fools still learning:
It's what school is all about.

THE 8.55

A whistle starts the 8.55,
Stops and destination unknown.
Sitting with backs to the engine,
Just kids
Who did not ask to be there.

The man who blew the whistle
Is not like them; not someone
With parents, pets, pimples,
A birthday,
A fondness for ice cream, a fear
Of heights – a fool at times
Who swaps jokes and secrets:
Just a teacher
Who gets off at the next stop
  –   Or stays on board for ever.

IT WAS SUMMER AND SUNDAY

Gingerly he picked up the putrescent egg,
The kind no rat would touch.
It was sickly green like the mouldy growth
On rotting trees – or cheese – or both.
A rat that ate it was a rat soon dead.
'I'll chuck it at whoever comes by,' he said.

A joke? Well, yes – from anyone else;
You could never be sure from his eyes:
Not quite the eyes of a playful child! –
Innocent enough when he smiled,
But when mouth stopped smiling eyes carried on
 – As on that day. Those strange eyes shone.

The immediate need? – to block retreat,
To tell him he would not dare. Not dare?
Wartime. For *horrid egg* read *hand grenade,*
For *boyish lark* read *commando raid.*
A hedge for cover, a lone lane ahead;
'The first to come past,' was all he said.

Pirate eyes scanned that empty lane,
Eager eyes for the sacrifice.
Then a moving blob came into view
With the face of a woman, a face we knew.
'Cor, it's Miss Fisk!' A giggle, a groan.
Miss Fisk of the infants'. Egg unthrown.

Closer the footsteps. 'Down, get down!'
Closer… like a scene from a film.

An arm drew back. A cricketer's fling.
A deadly aim. Like a stone from a sling.
Crack! on her shoulder, oozing green slime:
The Slapstick Moment – etched on time.

Funny thing, laughter, or sometimes so.
She turned and the mad laughter died.
Pretty young teacher, face all wet –
Real adult tears, hard to forget.
It was summer and Sunday. Smartly dressed,
She was off to meet someone, looking her best.

'Will you wipe this… mess from my coat?' –
(Sickly green like a mouldy growth.)
No, it's still there, now as then –
All the king's horses and all the king's men…
    Decades too late, but all the same:
Sorry, Miss Fisk. That was her real name.